The Easter Story

Song Titles:

1 The Easter Story 2 For God So Loved The World • John 3:16 3 Come Bless The Lord / Jesus In The Morning 4 Love, Love 5 Blessed Be The Name / Ho, Ho, Ho, Hosanna 6 When I Survey The Wondrous Cross 7 Alive, Alive 8 And Can It Be? 9 No Other Name But Jesus • Acts 4:12 10 When We All Get To Heaven 11 May Jesus Christ Be Praised / All Hail The Power 12 Everybody Ought To Know / He Is Lord 13 The Easter Story— With Page Turn Cues

To print the lyrics PDF, insert the CD into the computer drive. Click on START and then MY COMPUTER. Right-click on the CD drive and select OPEN from the drop down menu. Open the PDF documents like you open any other folder or file.

MW01144477

Jesus had told His closest friends that soon He would die but that on the third day He would be alive again. They did not remember Jesus' words. But the time came for Jesus' words to come true.

On Sunday, Jesus sent two disciples into a little village. "You will find a donkey which no one has ever ridden. Bring the donkey to Me," Jesus said.
"If someone asks what you are doing, say 'The Lord needs the donkey!'"
The disciples obeyed Jesus and brought the donkey to Him.

Jesus sat on the little donkey and together with His friends they headed toward the city of Jerusalem. Crowds of people stood along the side of the road.

They waved large palm branches and shouted, "**Hosanna! Blessed is He who comes in the name of the Lord**!"

On Monday, Jesus went into the temple in Jerusalem. He became very angry because the crowds of people were buying and selling animals—the people were not worshipping God.

So Jesus turned over their tables and made the buyers and sellers leave the temple. The religious leaders were upset with Jesus.

On Thursday evening, Jesus and His twelve disciples celebrated the Passover together. During the meal Jesus took some bread, prayed, and then gave some to His friends. "**This is My body**," He said, "which will be broken."

Then Jesus took the cup of wine, prayed, and gave some to His friends.
"**This is My blood**," He said. "I am giving you a new commandment:
Love one another so that everyone will know you are My disciples."

After the Passover meal, Jesus and His friends went into a nearby garden.
"Stay here and pray," Jesus said. "Please stay awake and pray for Me."
Jesus walked further into the garden, knelt on the ground, and began to pray.
"**Father, I am willing to do what You want**," Jesus said.

Soon a group of people and soldiers came through the garden carrying torches. Judas, one of Jesus' closest friends, was leading the way. The religious leaders gave him thirty pieces of silver if he would take them to Jesus.
The soldiers arrested Jesus.

The soldiers and religious leaders took Jesus to Pontius Pilate, a governor and a judge. Many people lied to the judge about the things Jesus had said and done. "**I find no wrong in this man. Let Jesus go**," said Pilate. But the crowd insisted that Jesus be crucified. Even though Pilate did not agree, he listened to the crowd.

Jesus was silent as the soldiers took Him away. They put on Jesus' head a crown made of thorns. The soldiers nailed Jesus to a cross. Jesus was heard praying, "**Father, forgive them**." Even though it was daytime, the skies grew dark for three hours. Jesus said in a loud voice, "**It is finished**!" and then He died.

Friends of Jesus placed His body in a tomb. A large stone was rolled in front of the entrance. Soldiers guarded the tomb so that no one would take Jesus' body

On Sunday morning, two women both named Mary came to the tomb. They found the stone rolled away from the entrance. An angel sitting on the stone said, "**Jesus is not here! He is alive**! Go quickly and tell His friends!" The women ran back to the others! "Jesus is alive! He is risen!" shouted the women. The friends did not believe the women! Peter, one of Jesus' closest friends, ran to the tomb. He looked inside and found only the cloths that had wrapped Jesus' body!

Later that day, Jesus joined two of His friends while they walked along the road to a little village. Then, Jesus visited the disciples in Jerusalem. He showed them His nail-scarred hands and feet! **It was true—Jesus was alive!**